# A Lionhearted Approach

# for Parent Coaching

An A-Z Guide for Taming Undesirable, Common
Toddler Behaviors (without the jargon!)

## Lisa Veshee

*"If you don't want to raise little
monsters, then read my book!"*

A Lionhearted Approach For Parent Coaching

An A-Z Guide for Taming Undesirable, Common Toddler Behaviors

Lisa Veshee

Book cover by: Antoinette Bastone

ISBN: 979-8-35092-755-9

Copyright Registration Number: TXu 2-386-814

# Table of Contents

# Dedication & Introduction

This book is dedicated to the families that I have been fortunate to have worked with and that gave me the opportunity to make a difference as a team! Many proposed the idea of writing this book to me; thank you for believing in me and inspiring me.

To my daughters, Jackie and Mackenzie, you've made me proud of the secure, confident, loving relationship that we have developed and continue to share and cherish. With continued love and support forever; we make a superb team!

My name is Lisa Veshee and I have been in the field of education for over thirty-five years: I am a New York State Certified Special Education Teacher: K-12/ Elementary Education Teacher: K-6, owned and directed Teetertots Daycare, a licensed Suffolk County Child Care Council facility for seven years, and have raised two children. For the last fifteen years, I have been an Early Intervention (Birth-3) special educator, parent coach, Applied Behavior Analysis (ABA) provider for families within: their homes, in preschools, and in daycares. I've learned some things along the way about behaviors and some ways to modify them. With the encouragement of my past and present families, I'd like to introduce discipline strategies for: parents, teachers, caregivers and the like. For the purposes of this book, I will refer to the word "parent" as the target word for the audience. The focus age range that I have the most experience with and will target for the purposes of this book is the toddler years. It is a child's job to push buttons, test boundaries, repeat undesired behaviors, whine, etc. It is the parent's job to set boundaries, be consistent, and follow through. I will provide easy to follow directions, without jargon, so you can practice effective strategies to combat undesired behaviors. For the purposes of this book, I will focus on the behavioral aspect of a child after ruling out any neurological or health factors. Welcome to the A–Z discipline book, (without the jargon); titled *A Lionhearted Approach to Parent Coaching*. YOU'VE GOT THIS!!!

> *Let's define discipline; it is not punishing and controlling but rather **teaching** children to be responsible for their actions and learning self-control. By teaching self-soothing skills and employing calm leadership and consistent discipline, your child will learn about consequences and be able to take responsibility for their own actions. I've never met a family that doesn't want a tranquil, happy family life. Some families need assistance in this domain; read on!

# A

## Accountability

Children should be held accountable for their actions. If a child dumps their toys, after completion of playing, they need to clean up after themselves. If they throw an object, have them retrieve the object and bring it back to the original spot from where it was thrown or put it in its right place. If they hurt someone, there needs to be a consequence. Asking children to say "sorry" is tricky due to the fact that one cannot control whether a child can speak or not. You can't force a child to speak but you can provide hand over hand support to rub the spot where the hit was administered, thereby making an attempt to soothe the wound and by showing appropriate touching. If you promised your child ice cream for cleaning up or acted appropriately in the store and they did not earn the ice cream, you can say; "I wanted to get ice cream, too, but you chose not to listen/clean up, etc. Maybe next time we can get ice cream." Demonstrate that it was the child's decision, not yours, that led to no ice cream but there's always a next time; put the decision to fix it in the child's control. Your child will do the best that they can to change your mind by crying and maybe even saying, "Sorry." Do not give in; your child will be very angry that they are not getting the reward at that time but will remember that you didn't give in, and the next time, you can remind them that they will not get the ice cream if they don't follow directions. There is a saying: Mean what you say, and say what you mean. Stick to your words, and be consistent. That's the only way to provide accountability.

## Anger

Children get angry, just like adults. It is what typically accompanies the anger that needs to be addressed. It is important that as a parent, you validate their feelings by saying, "I see that you're angry but you are not allowed to: hit, destroy objects, throw toys, etc." Sometimes anger needs to be released. Make it functional for them—they can hit a punching bag, scream into a pillow, sing aloud or exercise. These ideas may be some ways to appropriately release anger in children.

## Anticipating children's needs

For those families that have children with language delays or for those who would like to foster independence, stop anticipating your child's needs. Have children ask for a drink if they're thirsty or for something to eat if they're hungry. Even if they are unable to say the word, accept any utterance, provide praise, and use the correct word when giving the item. Children can communicate in many different ways: by using their words, physically taking the parent to the kitchen, pantry, or refrigerator. You can use visual boards: point to a picture. Take pictures of the foods they eat and place them in the vicinity of where it will be obtained, and have the child point to the desired item. This is called pairing. When the child points to the picture, the parent will vocalize the item for them and present it at the same time, by saying, "Nice job showing me that you want a cookie, juice, etc."

## "As soon as"

Some children are not ready for the word "no!" There is an alternative: "As soon as . . ."

"Mom, can I have a snack?" "Yes, AS SOON AS . . ." (you clean the blocks up), (you finish your homework,) whatever the task or desired behavior is. Use the terminology to have the child perform the targeted activity before the reinforcement is given. Make sure the desired behavior is displayed before the reward is given. You may offer assistance but don't do it for them; give them a chance to succeed!

## Attention

Children thrive on attention. Please give it to them in a positive way because if you don't, they may do something inappropriate to make sure you pay attention to them—even if it's in a negative way by yelling at them, it's attention regardless in their eyes. It doesn't have to be all day every day, but take time to play/read with your children. If your child wants to be in the kitchen with you, give them an easy task. Let them wash the fruit, or give them a towel and let them wipe the counters. Your child just wants to be a part of your day-to-day activities at times.

## Audience

All children throw tantrums—it's a part of the developmental process. It's the way parents handle the tantrums that may determine the severity and length of them. Typically, if there is no audience, then there will be nothing to gain from the performance. It has been my experience that when a child is throwing a tantrum, it's extremely effective to simply walk away, go into the other room, even pretend to answer the phone and start talking, or narrate aloud what you're doing (as long as they are not hurting themselves.) In other words, take your attention away from the child and place your attention on anything else. The more you try to soothe the child throwing a tantrum, the louder they get. Think about it: if you're angry and your spouse/friend tells you to calm down, do you? Most likely, you may get louder. When you see your child start to calm down (developing coping skills on their own), when they are no longer crying/yelling, address them by saying, "I really like the way you're calming down." Use any terminology you'd like but it's important to address the child when they are calm and pay no attention to them when they are vocally inappropriate.

## Barking orders

Having the opportunity to observe families and how they speak to each other in their natural environment gives me an advantage to evaluate the ways in which family members communicate with each other. I have seen children and parents alike yell or "bark" out one word responses when asked a simple question or what they wanted. If this pattern is allowed to continue, it becomes the norm. Every family has a different set of moral values. If you're not going to ask for "please" and "thank you," then at the least request a two to three-word sentence.

## Bedtime routine

Individuals of all ages come to rely on routines. It reduces stress and makes people feel comfortable knowing what happens next. This is especially true for children. Have a routine for evenings, this will assist in reducing tantrums and receiving more compliance. Stick to the same routine as much as possible. For example, eat dinner, watch TV for half-an-hour, bath, brush teeth, book, bed, etc.

# Behavior

Behavior is a form of communication, always remember that! Children (it doesn't stop there) throw tantrums/cry for a reason. Parents attempt to figure that out from the moment of birth. Infants have a certain cry for hunger, pain, sickness, feeling tired, etc. Why stop trying to figure it out when they become toddlers? Lack of a toddler's ability to convey their thoughts, feelings, fear, anxiety, etc., may be an apparent reason. Pay attention and think about the moment before a child throws a tantrum (antecedent.) Was it because you said "no?" Was it due to a lack of ability to express wants and needs? You're not paying attention to them? Are they overstimulated? Are they tired? They are conveying in the only way they know how to—through their behavior. Again, keep in mind that behavior is a form of communication. This will assist in developing the mindset of parenting skills needed to decipher the reason before you may come up with a plan or to be able to stop the behavior before it starts. Look at patterns to see when the behaviors occur. This will help to find out the reason for it.

# Biting

Biting is a common undesired behavior of toddlers. Typically, it will pass. Putting all the attention on the "victim" rather than the biter him/herself has proven to be successful, in most cases, to eliminate this behavior. Use words for the biter (that they cannot express themselves) to express sorrow: "Oh, I am so sorry that ( . . . ) bit you!!" Pay no attention to the biter; you can even go as far as fetching a Band-Aid and making a dramatic scene (which would be highly effective) and placing it on the wound of the victim, while continuing to place attention on the wounded soul. Do not place any emphasis on the biter; especially not to apologize to the person they bit, that puts the child who bit in control.

## Body language

It is important to read your child's body language. If a child walks to the other side of the house and it's not to avoid a given instruction then let them. I had a mom who kept bringing her son back to the spot from where he originally walked away, and he started getting physical. In this case, the child was clearly exhibiting a desire to be alone and away from the situation. Individuals need space at times and that needs to be respected. As long as the child is safe, let them practice self-soothing/coping skills without intervention.

## Boundaries

Children thrive on boundaries but fight them every step of the way; it is their nature! It is the parent's responsibility to be consistent in following through with requests, even if it means using "physical assistance" to help in the process. By that, I mean literally taking your hand and putting it over your child's hand and performing the desired action. While asking a child to pick up a thrown object, give your child an opportunity to comply with the original request. If they do not listen, then apply the hand over hand technique, without words, until the objects are cleaned up. There are many homes I've been to where the shelves are bare because their children take any and all decorations off the shelves. Use the terminology: "That's Mommy's decorations, you cannot play with (object), this is your toy; you can play with this." It is imperative that your child knows and understands what they can and cannot touch at home, which should also apply to your guest's home while on an outing.

# C

## Choices

Giving reasonable choices between two distinct objects is a good way to foster a child's independence. If you ask your child what they want to wear for the day or what they would like for a snack and display the entire closet or cabinet filled with snacks; that is too overwhelming for a child. Keep it simple—hold an object in each hand or display two pictures of the items, and ask, "Which one?" Have your child practice pointing or labeling the object or have them ask for the desired object in a sentence, whichever is preferred by the parent. If you want your child to put their coat on before taking them to preschool, the choice is: "Put your coat on or I will help you," not "Put your coat on or we're not leaving." The ultimate goal is to have your child comply with the original request. Give them an opportunity to do so independently or you will have to help them by putting it on for them. Whether your child protests or not, once you give a request, it needs to be followed through. Keep in mind that sometimes we have choices and sometimes we don't. It is up to the parents to decide when choices are appropriate and when they're not.

## Choose your battles

Ask yourself, does this behavior interfere with a functional lifestyle? If it does not, then leave it alone. If it does, then it's a choice to change the undesired behavior. You can't go after all the behaviors at once. Pick the one that's most bothersome and tackle that one first, then the next one and so on.

## Coming to the speaker

Do not chase your children. Call their name and have them come to you instead. This starts with practice. Say, "(Child's name) come here." If they don't listen, go to them and bring them to you as you say, "When I call your name, I need you to come to me." Practice this so that children will be able to apply this to all situations.

## Consequences

For consequences to be effective, they have to be immediate. You need to follow through and there needs to be consistency. Consequences need to make sense. For example, do say, "If you don't turn off your computer (within five minutes), I am going to take it away for the rest of the evening (whatever duration the parent decides.)" Don't say, "If you don't turn off your computer (within five minutes), I'm going to throw it out the window!" In other words, mean what you say and follow through on your consequence. Take away the computer if the child does not comply with the request within the time allotted! If you're asking your child to clean up before leaving the house for an outing, then sit down and wait until they clean up before leaving the house (delaying their exciting time going out.) The ultimate goal is for the child to comply with a request, which means at times they may require "assistance." Always give the child an opportunity to succeed independently. For example, if you're asking a child to get dressed or any other skill that they are capable of but may be unwilling to perform, then you can say, "If you don't get dressed by yourself, I can help you." It is a good idea to count to three to give your child time to decide to comply with the initial request independently. On three, you are walking to your child and assisting them in the original task that was requested in a calm manner without words. It is likely that when a parent decides to begin to administer consequences to get rid of undesired behaviors, the behavior will increase (due to the sudden change in the parent's behavior) but with consistency, the behaviors will decrease. Read the soda machine analogy for a perspective.

My friend, J.P., shared a great analogy—she calls it the Soda Machine Analogy. You push the button and get the soda, that's what's expected. Suddenly, one day you put money in the machine and select the desired soda. You push the button and don't get the soda, so yell at the machine, or kick and slam the machine to try to get the soda to drop. When you realize that it won't work, you accept your fate and walk away.

## Consistency

Did your child ever look directly at you while they were doing something they knew they weren't supposed to do? They are looking to see if you will respond the same way each time. I phrase it this way—it's a child's job to test their parents; it's the parents' job to be consistent each and every time. If you are consistent, the behavior will most likely decrease before disappearing altogether. We'll use the example of jumping on the couch. You're in the living room and your child looks at you while he climbs on the couch and starts jumping. You say, "Get down." Your child continues to jump. At this point, you can ask again and if the jumping continues, you walk over to the child and pick him/her up and place them in front of something they can engage in. Inevitability, the child will jump on the couch again and it's your job to react the same way. The one time you're too tired or not in the mood to deal with the behavior, it will take longer to combat the jumping.

## Coping skills

Please stop trying to fix everything for your child or trying to make everything better so they don't cry or get upset. Children need to learn how to cope with disappointments. I'm not talking about if they get hurt—of course, you soothe them and render care. I'm talking about when they are not able to get what they want or if instant gratification is not instant enough. Validate their feelings by letting them be upset—it will push them to self-soothe, and in doing so, it is teaching coping skills that are necessary for a well-balanced, happy individual.

## Cutting nails

Many parents I talk to try to cut their children's nails while they are asleep. If you are unable to do so and your child is noncompliant during this necessary grooming session, then here are some suggestions. Try to desensitize them by not cutting, but simply taking the nail clippers and tapping their nails. You can even give them the clippers to tap their own nails. You can also have an incentive—a wrapped toy as a reward at the beginning of the process and fade back the rewards as the child complies.

# *D*

## Danger

By approximately three years of age, a child should be able to avoid common dangers (sharp knives, fire, or a hot stove.) A strategy to use beforehand would be to replicate a picture of a stop sign or have a simple red piece of paper indicating to STOP where there may be potential danger. Children have been passengers in cars since they were infants and probably know what a stop sign is by the time they're walking. This "stop sign" replica may be placed by the front door, so as not to walk out of the house, at the top of the stairs, on the stove, by the pool, or any place that might present a dangerous situation. It can serve as a visual reminder.

## Diaper changing

It is typical that as toddlers start exerting some independence, they may fight diaper changes. They may not want to be taken away from playtime, they're on the go, or simply asserting independence. Some strategies to help with this: give advanced notification by saying, "In two minutes, we're going to change your diaper." Provide a distraction—give your child a toy, the iPad, or make it fun by having a special song or book to accompany the process. Switch it up, change your child standing up or in a different location to extinguish patterned behavior.

| Do | Don't |
|---|---|
| Be firm | Yell |
| Be a parent | Be your child's friend |
| Listen to your child | Judge them |
| Set boundaries and be respected | Let your children ignore your requests |
| Frolic play | Let it escalate |
| Give a consequence | Lock them in their room |
| Say "goodbye" when dropping your child off | Don't sneak away |
| Celebrate your child's individual accomplishments | Compare them to others |

## Do not sneak out of the house

Say goodbye to your child. If you sneak out of the house when your child is not looking, it may create anxiety for the child. Think about it. You're there one minute and when the child turns around the next and you're gone, it can be scary. This could result in the child following you around all the time (because they want to make sure you don't disappear) and crying if you're not in their field of vision all the time. Say goodbye to your child when you leave the house, drop them off at daycare or at a sitter's house. Tell them that you'll be back later to pick them up and then leave. Don't linger and keep going back time after time for one more kiss—just say goodbye and leave. This is one good way for your child to develop coping skills.

## Domain

Typically speaking, your child feels most comfortable within their own surroundings/domain. This is where they feel that they can be at their best and worst without being judged, knowing that they are unconditionally loved. Often toddlers "hold it together" while they are in daycare, preschool, or somewhere else other than home during the day. When they get home, they may inadvertently unleash the control they fought so hard to maintain during the day. Keep this in mind when dropping off your child. Say "goodbye" and then leave without turning around too many times and when picking them up, don't linger more than you have to upon picking them up. Children are generally anxious to get home.

## Dressing

Sometimes parents are on a tight schedule in the morning as they are getting ready for work, taking care of other siblings, or would just like a smooth morning routine. Part of starting your day is getting dressed. If your child gives you a hard time dressing, you can try these strategies: holding up two different shirts/pants/dresses and asking, "Which one?" This allows them to choose, which gives them certain control but also the obligation to put it on. You can try picking out an outfit the night before, or in the morning. Before any TV, iPad, or other incentive is given, the child must dress first.

## Dumping

Dumping things is a developmental stage that allows children to explore the world around them. It's fun for them and they get to see all the colors and hear the noise it makes. You can use a strategy to clean up by making it fun. Use a sorting activity—let's clean up all the cars, blue objects, dolls first, until it's all cleaned up. Before moving on the next activity, the dumped basket/bin should be cleaned up.

# E

## Eating

Children almost always eat whatever they are served; that is until around two years of age, when they start to develop likes and dislikes. This is also around the time when they start to gain control. One of the only ways that a child can have control is when they choose to eat or not. Unless it's a sensory issue, this is a phase and instead of telling your child to "eat," you can try different strategies such as ignoring the child at the table and not placing emphasis on eating. Instead you can remind them to "pick up their fork." Praise others for eating, don't stare at or watch over your child at the dinner table. This attention is a good way for them to rebel and not eat. You can have your child help with the preparation of the meal, have your child feed their doll/teddy bear first, then the child takes a bite, or blend up vegetables in order to hide them in order to fool your child into eating their veggies!

## Electronics

Many of the families I work with have electronic devices that their children use, whether it is the parent's phone, an iPad, or tablet. It's amazing how children, sometimes less than two years old, navigate these devices! It is highly recommended that screen time is monitored and limited. I have seen children have an all-out meltdown screaming, "iPad, iPad, iPad!" when the iPad is taken away. Give a verbal warning: "Two more minutes before you have to turn off, put aside, or hit the pause button." Practice having your child hit the pause button and put it to the side to engage in an activity or to eat, then resume screen time at the caregiver's, NOT the child's, liking. It is important to have the device within the child's sight while it is not being physically used— many parents hide the device because it causes a problem. This is a great opportunity to teach boundaries and to have children "wait."

## Expectation of behaviors

Explain to your child how you expect them to behave, whether it is an outing or in the bathtub (anyplace your child may have difficulties.) When you pull into the parking lot, before you get out of the car, tell your child, "When you hear me calling your name, you need to come to me." "When it's time to leave the park, I expect you to hold my hand," "When we're in the store, no running away from me." If the child is old enough, have him/her repeat the "terms" before getting out of the car. Have the child agree to the terms before you get out of the car or go into the restaurant, park, etc. Explain the consequences of not keeping up their part of the bargain; you'll have to remove the child immediately from the environment if they do not adhere to the terms discussed before they got out of the car. It is imperative that there are no second chances. This way the child will clearly understand that you are the one in control. Chances are you will take the child out of the situation kicking and screaming but the benefits will far outweigh that one, or it may take two or three tries. If you are calm and consistent, the child will listen to you and you may not have any issues going forward.

## Fighting siblings

It is inevitable that siblings will fight over their toys, attention, space, and other factors. Ideally, it would be nice if siblings were friends but that doesn't happen till much later. It is usually the younger sibling getting in the older sibling's way because that's just the way it is—they want to be like their older brother/sister. In many ways and the older sibling may feel that since the younger one came along, everything is "ruined," and may be resentful at first so try to be sensitive to this. Make an effort to discipline the younger sibling in front of the older one, by saying, "You're not allowed to grab from your sister/brother," "No pulling hair," "This is your sister/brother's time with mommy." Even if the younger sibling is an infant, it will validate the older one's feelings. When children are older and they are arguing, stop them and have them say something nice to each other while looking into each other's eyes. It's difficult to do when they are angry but it puts a positive spin on their feelings. Under no circumstances should a parent tolerate physical fighting. Immediate consequences on both parties should be handed out; a motivating incentive should be withheld and children need to be separated. Let them know in a stern voice that physical violence is not allowed in your home.

## Following directions

When asking your child to perform a certain task; for example: getting his/her shoes, throwing out an object, putting their dish in the sink after dinner, cleaning up their toys; whatever the direction is, if the child does not comply, you need to physically help them by either escorting them to the destination or putting your hand over theirs and performing the activity together (hand over hand.) All the while, tell them, "This is how you (fill in the blank.)" Be consistent with physically assisting them if you're asking them to do something and you are being ignored.

## Follow through

When you say to a child before going to the playground, "You need to come to me when I call your name, or we'll have to leave the park" and you call them and they don't come to you, you need to leave the park. That holds true in the case of each and every direction that is made by you Such as, "Clean up your toys before going outside to play." If you're inconsistent with following through with your consequences ("No outside until the toys are cleaned up"), it relays the message that the child does not have to listen. If you say something, mean it.

## Gaining control

As the head of household, you, the parent, are in control of reversing undesirable behaviors with your child. Don't walk on eggshells around your children, or be afraid of having your child be "mad" at you. I can almost assure you, children will not hold a grudge if you set boundaries and follow through. In fact, they're more likely to respect you. Be one step ahead of your children. You know your children and you know what "sets them off." Be one step ahead of them then. If you know that your child is going to run away from you in the store, have a firm grip on their hand to prevent it from happening. If your child opens the kitchen drawers, get locks for them. If you know your child won't come inside when it's time, be in their vicinity when you call their name, and if they choose to run, you'll be there to redirect them into following your direction.

# H

## Haircuts

Having a haircut can be traumatic, especially for young boys who require a buzzer and a trimmer as well. A good way to prepare for the haircut experience is to desensitize your child to the equipment. If possible, purchase an inexpensive buzzer and have your child turn it on and off many times as a way of controlling the device. Have the child experience the buzzer by placing it on their leg or arm intermittently and gradually move towards the head, all the while having control of turning off the buzzer at any given time. Have your child buzz cut one of his stuffed animals or cars and praise the object for their bravery and compliance. You can purchase a small toy or a lollipop as a reward to be given after the completion of the haircut. Keep the reward in sight or in the child's hands (unopened) until the cut is complete.

## Hand over hand

Hand over hand is the act of placing your hands over the child's hand in order to comply with a request if they are unwilling to do so independently. This can be applied in situations where a parent is asking the child to perform a simple task and they do not comply. Cleaning up after activities is a good example. The parent asks the child to clean up and the child simply walks away or says "no." It's a good idea to give the child a chance to comply on his/her own first before asking if they need "help." That's where the parent will put his hand over the child's hand and clean up together and may sing the clean up song as a diversion or say no words at all—the choice is the caregiver's. Whatever the request, if the child does not comply, hand over hand is necessary to let the child know that if a request is made, it will be followed even if assistance is needed. This will let the child know that he may as well complete the task on his own in the future; otherwise it will be done anyway with the assistance of the hand over hand technique.

## Have fun with your child

There are so many opportunities to have fun and to have different experiences with your child. Everything should not be a teachable moment. Take time to enjoy your children and to the best of your abilities, give them exposure to various platforms and encourage playful nonrestrictive time to explore at their leisure. Laugh, be silly, engage with them as they crave your attention.

## Help

Help means "help," not "doing it for them." As a whole, parents do not like to see their children struggle. In fact, many intervene before a child has a chance to either succeed or ask for help. As long as there is no danger to the child, sit back a little and watch as your child struggles with a task. It's a chance at developing coping skills, patience, self-correcting, and a way to manage their abilities in a creative way. If it becomes too challenging, prompt your child to ask for "help" instead of them grunting or crying out. Then assist them. Most often, parents take over the task, as children lean out of the way. Be mindful of that and assist only as much as they need, instead of doing the task for them. They will most likely feel so much better and will experience a sense of accomplishment once they have achieved the task. That will boost self-confidence and self-worth.

## If/then contingency plan

One way to have your child comply with requests is to enforce the if/then contingency plan (the Premack Principle.) Here are some examples: If (you eat your dinner), then (you can have dessert.) If you (finish your homework), then (you can watch TV.) If (you clean up your toys), then (you can go outside.) Fill in the blanks as necessary and don't forget the key factor: Be consistent with following through on the contingency plan, even if it may require hand over hand (discussed above) assistance. We are rooting for your child to succeed in any way possible.

## Isolation/locking them in their room

Children who require a consequence for their behavior do not need to be put in a space where they are isolated. This may cause a sense of anxiety and fear, and can be detrimental to their psyche. There will most likely be a spike in their verbal response when thrown into that situation and it's most likely due to being put in that situation. A better strategy would be to either allow them a quiet space to decompress if needed, without forcing isolation on them. Or try the planned ignoring strategy coupled with narrating your actions aloud. Pay no attention to your child's behavior as you talk aloud the activities you are doing: "Oh, I forgot to empty the dishwasher; let me put the plates in the cabinet, the knives go in this drawer, etc." This is a good way to change an undesired behavior.

Just breathe. Raising children is an additional job if you happen to be working outside the home. It's a full-time job if you're a stay-at-home mom/dad. Everything gets done; this is not the time to keep a perfect house, rather it's a home. The days may be long but the time goes very fast.

## Jealousy

Most children enjoy being the center of attention. Oftentimes when I am discussing with adult family members about the session I just had with their child, their sibling gets very loud or will ask the person I'm speaking to for a desired object or start climbing on them. More often than not, the adult I'm speaking to ignores this behavior and it is left to me to address the situation. I stop talking and tell the attention seeker that I am talking and that they need to wait for whatever it is they want. This is all part of discipline and it needs to be addressed immediately so it will not continue. At times, I also see older children get jealous of the younger siblings, and sometimes they say, "I don't like (name)" or "I wish (name) was never born." That's when you talk to your older child about family morals and values. Remember to give equal attention as best as possible, spend some quality time with the older sibling while the younger one is napping or when the younger one goes to bed. This should help with jealousy issues; it's difficult growing up!

## Just breathe

Enjoy your children; not everything is a complication or a task that needs to be met. Take time to enjoy the process; time goes quickly. The days can be long but time is short; practice patience and validation when necessary.

## Know your audience

Each child is an individual with likes and dislikes. I wouldn't bring my daughter to a snake exhibit because she's terrified of them but my nephew would really enjoy going. While I am in session with my students, I think about what would motivate them and try to run my lessons based on their likes because it would be a much more effective session; especially upon meeting them for the first time. Objects can be adaptable. While working on matching colors, you can use whatever motivates the learner—dinosaurs, balls, crowns, etc.

## Less is more

Keep it simple and minimal when it comes to verbal discipline. I've heard some parents of my students say: "Stop jumping on the couch because if you fall, you can get hurt and may have to go to the hospital." The correct response should be: "Get down" or "No jumping," as you physically assist them off the couch and onto the floor and to something they can engage in. If you keep going on and on, the message gets lost. Some children have an abundance of toys and they are all over the living room or in their bedroom; this can be overstimulating for children. Fill two or three bins with toys each week and switch out the toys, so the child can explore without being surrounded by too many toys.

## Learned behavior

Examples of learned behavior include the following: A child wants a toy in the store and cries until he/she gets it. A child grunts loudly instead of asking for help, and a parent comes over and fixes the problem. A child comes to you upon hearing his/her name called, etc.

Children learn that certain behaviors they display can result in getting them whatever they want. When left uncorrected, these undesirable behaviors will increase. The longer you wait, the longer it will take to change the behavior. The ultimate goal is for the child to develop appropriate learned behaviors instead of undesired ones. Again, being consistent and setting boundaries will make this happen.

## Learning styles

According to Neil Fleming's <u>VARK</u> (Visual, Auditory, Reading, Kinesthetic) model, individual learning falls into various categories. This means that students of all ages have preferred learning styles. These styles can influence learning and behavior. In order for a learner to thrive, their environment should match their particular learning style. There is no one particular style and your child may have a combination of styles. Therefore noting the importance of knowing that they exist will help you better understand your child's thought process.

<u>V</u>isual learning style:
These types of learners prefer and learn best when they see: charts, graphics, diagrams, maps, and other graphical materials. Videos and PowerPoint presentations can also help these learners. Strict reliance on text and words is not going to work to the strength of this type of learner. This kind of learner does well with symbols of relationships, as with a flow chart, picture, or diagram representing a process.

Auditory learning style
These kinds of learners learn best when they hear or speak. They like lectures, learning from a radio broadcast, mobile phone learning, IPad videos, and talking in groups. Talking out loud can also help this learner.

Read/write learning style
Words are what learners who prefer this learning style like. This can include all kinds of reading, including reports, newspaper articles, essays, assignments, and manuals. Many individuals in this category like: PowerPoint presentations, web presentations, dictionaries, and any medium where words are important.

Kinesthetic (hands on/tactile) learning style
Those who prefer this learning style like a connection to reality. This can be through simulations, examples, or experiences (getting down and dirty!). Reading about baking cookies would not be as good as actually putting all the ingredients together and baking them using a hands on approach. These learners do react well to demonstrations, movies, and videos of real things. Simply put, these learners learn well when they do things.

## Listening

Many toddlers have what's called selective hearing. If a child is engaged in a fun activity and you call their name: "Johnny, come here," chances are, they will go on playing. You can stop this pattern of ignoring your request by calling their name once, maybe twice, and by the third time, say the child's name, and walk towards them. Take them by the hand and bring them to the original spot where you were when you started calling their name. Say, "When I call your name, I expect you to come to me." If you give a child a request and they don't listen to you, then hand over hand is necessary to comply with your request, and as always, consistency is key.

# M

## Meltdown

"Meltdown" is another word for having a tantrum. One way to combat a meltdown is to be one step ahead of your child. If you know that your child is going to cry when he sees his sneakers by the door (because he'll want to go outside to play), make sure they're out of sight. If your child opens the cabinet and wants snacks, only put the snacks that you are willing to have him eat instead of battling what he can and cannot eat. We cannot always be one step ahead of a meltdown; so, when it happens, the one golden rule is to NEVER engage with your child while they are having a meltdown (Refer to Planned ignoring.) As soon as your child is quiet, you may dote all attention on them.

## Modeling

Children model (copy) what they see, whether it's appropriate language/behavior or inappropriate language/behavior. Show them how to act as you go about your daily routine. Your children are watching you! Be a kind, helpful, respectful person; exercise and eat right, they will be more inclined to do the same. Show them how to treat the family pet and other individuals. While playing a game with them, show them the appropriate way to win or lose. Or if they're building a tower of blocks and it falls down, tell them that it's ok, just start over!

# N

## Nail cutting

For those of you that sneak into your child's room while they're sleeping and are able to cut their nails without incident, that works. However, it is not addressing the fact that your child needs to be able to allow you to cut their nails as a matter of hygiene, and as a willing, active participant. Strategies include: having your child cut the nails of his favorite stuffed animal or character. He can practice cutting his animal or character's nails first; then it's his turn. Consider praising the brave character that is going first to hype up the child into wanting to go next. Desensitizing is another alternative; without intending to cut your child's nails that day, have the clippers visually present. Periodically tap the child's nails without attempting to actually cut them. Get your child used to the presence of the tool without being afraid of it. Then talk to them and let them know while you're tapping the fingernails that not today, but soon you will actually clip their nails going forward.

# No

Some children are not quite ready to hear the word "no." If a child is grabbing an object that you don't want them to have, give them something they can have, instead of saying "no." In other words, "You can't have (my phone) but can have (his toy.)" Physically replace the preferred object while taking away the non-preferred one—a swap if you will. As discussed earlier, "as soon as," is another alternative to saying "no."

There are times of course when "no" needs to be heard, especially in a dangerous situation such as touching a hot stove, running in the parking lot, and not listening to you as you try to redirect them from doing something they're not supposed to be doing. If you use the term "no," use it in a firm voice with as few words as possible: "No jumping" (on the couch), "no hitting," "no biting," "no throwing." Most of the time we need to actually say "no" is when they are performing an unwanted action. It is important to use as few words as possible and to be firm.

# O

## Object retrieval

This is a great way to gain your child's confidence and expand their vocabulary. Mostly when you're on your way out the door, you typically grab your child's socks/shoes and put them on your child. You may have to get a coat/sweatshirt, a snack, etc. Have your child be an active participant in this process. Does your child know that a shoe is actually a shoe? That a sock, is a sock? It's important to label everyday objects so that your child understands that words have meaning. Ask your child to go get his socks and shoes. You may have to show him/her the first time by physically walking them to their room, going to the sock drawer, and getting the socks before closing the drawer, same thing with their shoes and jacket. You can do this with diapers, clothes, toys, and food/drink. This is another way of gaining independence as well. You can praise your child for being such a "big helper" and watch his face light up!

## On their time

I've heard parents ask, "Why isn't my son/daughter potty-trained?" Fill in the action with any phrase or developmentally appropriate milestone. Children learn in many different ways and not all at the same level. Introduce new concepts as the child learns to master a previous skill. Be patient and understand the way your child best retains information (see Learning styles above.) Provide examples by modeling and narrating actions. Let your child practice and make mistakes. This is an important step in learning to be independent, practicing patience, and solving problems. Don't berate them by saying, "You should be doing this by now," or "why can't you just do it?" Be encouraging and lend support when necessary.

## Ownership

Children need to be accountable for their actions. For example, if you call your child's name at the park and they don't come to you upon hearing their name (this is discussed prior to entering the park), then it's time to leave. When your child cries and yells that they don't want to leave, then you can calmly say, "I wanted to stay at the park but you chose not to listen, so we have to leave. Maybe next time you will listen." If the ground rules are set beforehand, then there is no room for second chances—this leads to third and fourth chances which are not effective. Same if your child hits another child, if they are not acting appropriately or being generally non-compliant. You can say things like, "I wanted to (fill in the blank) but you chose to (fill in the blank)." You can then remind them that there will be a next time and hopefully they will make a better choice and the experience can last longer.

# P

## Pets

Pets are considered members of the family and need to be treated as such. This means that children need to be taught the correct way to handle them, which certainly does not include pulling the ears or tail and not locking the animal away from your child. Teach your child the correct way to pet and approach household pets. I tell parents that if your child is mistreating the pet and gets bitten, it's the child's fault and the animal ends up paying for it.

## Phone

Your phone is not a toy for your child to play with. I have experienced trying to reach someone and they don't respond because either their child was on the phone or their child erased the message. Not giving your child your phone is a way to set limits or boundaries that your child needs to follow. If they reach for your phone, give them something they can have instead. Very often when a parent gets a phone call, the child starts acting out and yelling to gain the parents' attention. It is important to set the boundary and tell your child that you're on the phone and that he/she needs to go play until you're done. This doesn't mean you can be on the phone for hours; be reasonable.

## Pinching

If your child pinches you or another family member, immediately turn them (your child) away as you stand up and walk away in an abrupt manner. If it continues, you can say, "No pinching," as you turn your child away and remove yourself from the situation in the same manner. This movement does not reinforce this action and your child will realize that when this behavior is displayed, it gets no attention; therefore, it should diminish.

## Planned ignoring

I like to use this technique especially when a child is crying or throwing a tantrum. The act of planned ignoring is as simple as what is stated—I plan on ignoring the child if he/she is crying or throwing a tantrum—crying in a behavioral sense rather than being hurt. Pay no attention to the child when they are screaming; attend to them only when they calm down. Think about it—if you are upset and ranting, do you want someone telling you to calm down or stop? No, you might get louder if someone interferes with your venting; it's the same with children. This is a perfect opportunity for them to develop self-soothing and coping skills. You can keep yourself busy so as to not look at your child. If there is no audience, there is less likely to be a performance. Narrate aloud while you're tidying up or pretend to get a phone call and even laugh aloud. If someone else is around; start talking to them, by saying, "Oh guess what I saw today . . ." Anything to direct your attention away from the crying toddler. The child can have all the attention you want to give when they are quiet!

## Pleading

I have witnessed parents pleading with their children to do as they request. "Please (put your socks and shoes on)", "Please (I'll give you a piece of candy, if you just fill in the blank)." Do not plead with your child; it gives them complete control over the situation. Instead use the Premack Principle and say, "If you (don't clean up your toys), then (we can't go to the park)." "If you don't let me put your shoes on, we can't go to McDonald's." Sometimes you simply need to go to the doctor's appointment or run an errand and your child just needs to comply with the simple request. Try to use an incentive to entice your child to comply with your request. If they do not comply with your request, simply say nothing and perform the task physically with them using hand over hand when necessary to complete the original request.

## Pointing in your child's face

It is demeaning to a child to have an adult yelling at them while a finger is pointed at their face. It may make them feel ashamed and embarrassed. There is no reason to humiliate a child when they make a mistake or misbehave.

# Potty training

As your child ages and grows into a toddler and beyond; your child will, at one time or another, transition from diapers to being potty trained. There is no one best way to teach your child to go on the potty. Your child will let you know when they are ready. They will begin to let you know their diaper is full and needs to be changed; they may start to hide away from you to have a bowel movement, or ask to be changed. There are some strategies that have worked successfully in the past. Have your child watch (model) appropriate actions in the bathroom. Let them pick out their own underwear with their favorite characters on them, use a small reward for when they are successful (sticker, stamp on the hand, piece of candy), put the potty chair in the playroom or near the bathroom and have your child sit on it intermittently, maybe with a book? You can implement a schedule, take them every forty-five minutes and chart when your child eliminates. Create a potty song for encouragement if your child is nervous. Place a small amount of dish soap which will create bubbles, how fun! Praise, praise, praise when they urinate in the potty! Never reprimand a child who accidentally urinates while wearing underwear. Remember making a bowel movement is scarier on the potty, so you may up the ante with rewards and patience.

# Praise

One of the most effective ways to foster the behavior you desire from your child is to praise your child for their efforts while they are learning a new task. Praise can come in a variety of ways; the most common being verbal praise. The only thing to keep in mind when using verbal praise is to be behavior-specific with your child's actions while praising. Instead of saying, "Good boy/girl," say, "I really like the way you (fill in the blank)," or "nice job doing (fill in the blank)." Fade back on the praising your child too much; as it becomes expected behavior once learned. Not every task a child performs needs to be praised every time. Saying "good boy/girl" does not specify the behavior you would like to continue—the child has no idea why they're being "good." Additionally, praise can be physical. Simply give a quick thumbs-up, a smile, a tousle of the hair, a wink, a hug, even an approving nod. Praise can be tactile: a sticker, a stamp, or a picture of a smiley face. Praise can be a special treat, extra time with video equipment, or anything that brings pleasure to your child.

## Pretend you don't see it

Children will repeat an undesired action or behavior to make sure you're going to respond the same way each and every time. They know they're not supposed to jump on the couch or touch the TV but they will do it right in front of you, sometimes with a smile, and watch for your reaction. That's when you may sometimes "pretend" you don't see them jumping or touching something they are not supposed to. It's not much fun when you don't react—and this may have them stop the behavior. The only time you can't pretend that you aren't seeing it is when they are in danger or are hurting a pet or sibling—those simply cannot be ignored, and a consequence needs to be given right away to let them know that physical violence will not be tolerated.

## Questions

Most toddlers are great with asking questions. Usually, they should be encouraged and happily answered so that your child gains knowledge. But sometimes, children will ask the same question over and over again. One way to deter this is to answer a question with a question. When a child asks, "When are we going to the park?" the first time you can tell them, "Right after lunch or after your nap." Try to be specific because they have difficulty with time intervals. Instead of saying to your child when they ask; "when are we leaving?" don't say; "in ten minutes," say, "after lunch." Most often your child will ask again, "When can we go to the park?" Your response should be, "When are we going to the park?" Answer the question with a question. You can prompt your child by saying, "When did I say we were going, you tell me?" If you have a special outing planned, such as a day at the beach, a birthday party, a trip to Grandma's, a playdate with a friend, or running errands, don't tell your child until approximately 20–30 minutes before you're going to leave. Otherwise, there's a good chance you will be inundated with the question: "When are we leaving?" which can turn into a tantrum if the child is made to wait too long.

## Quiet corner

In my experience, there are some homes that are overstimulating to children. There is an abundance of toys around with no organizational system, which creates chaos. Try to create a cozy quiet corner for your child to decompress and calm him/herself. Use oversized pillows and maybe a blanket. I've seen some quiet corners that have a teepee tent for the child as well. You can put books and stuffed animals in there or play soft music. It should be free from requests and designed to make your child feel relaxed and safe.

## Reinforcers

Would you work if you just got handed a paycheck for just showing up? Most people would say, "Of course not!" The paycheck is the reinforcer in this example. One works in order to gain money—it's a motivator for us to show up at our job. When you are asking a child to do something and they don't want to do it, try finding something that would motivate the child to perform the request. You can simply show them the reinforcing object or edible (food item) and let them know that if they (clean up their toys) they can use the iPad. Don't keep asking the child if they want the (iPad,) the reinforcer should make them jump up and do whatever was asked of them. If they don't, then you're not using the right reinforcer (motivator.) You can use the "if/then" or "first/then" contingency plan like we discussed earlier if your child needs a verbal instead of just visual prompt. "If you want the (iPad,) then clean up your toys." It is imperative that the reinforcer be given to the child immediately upon completion of the original request; don't add anything to the first request. When introducing reinforcers, the child needs to pair the reward (reinforcer) with the task. As the child gets familiar with the concept, you can add additional requests in order to gain the reinforcer. Eventually we get to the point where it is just a request and a response without having to be "paid."

## Routines

Children thrive on routines. When a routine is set in place, the child knows what to expect of them and is more apt to follow requests. With working parents, a morning routine is encouraged to make sure everyone gets out of the house on time. There is no guarantee that hiccups will not occur but in general, the morning will run a bit more smoothly when everyone knows their role, same with a nightly routine, especially during the week with school, daycare, and work. Weekends can be a bit more flexible, especially when a special occasion comes up. Routines can be posted either in writing or in the form of a visual with photographs next to time intervals and can be as elaborate or simple as possible. You can make a checklist for older children, which will encourage independence and boost confidence.

# S

## Scheduling

Scheduling is similar to routines, although the increments are for longer periods of time or blocks of time/days. Routines are mostly day-to-day activities, and schedules break down the child's day into time increments. As children thrive on routines, they thrive on schedules as well. Extracurricular activities may be part of your child's daily routine and can be a great way to interact with peers, learn appropriate social behavior, fulfill obligations, and keep them active. Sticking to a schedule may assist in keeping your child grounded as they know what's expected of them on any given day. If necessary, a visual schedule may be useful in assisting your child view the day ahead to reduce uncertainty. A checklist may also aid in the process. As your child completes a task, they can check it off their to-do list which assists in boosting self-esteem.

## Self-soothing

Inadvertently, some tantrum behaviors which include crying, yelling, and throwing him/herself to the floor may be accidentally reinforced.

Individuals that coddle or pick up children and try to soothe or stop them from crying may actually be getting in the way of a child's ability to have a crucial understanding of self-soothing. It has been discussed that when children start crying in order to gain attention, it's more effective to let them try to calm themselves down by gaining self-soothing tactics, thereby controlling their own behavior instead of relying on others to control it for them. This is obtained by 'planned ignoring' and the 'narrating aloud,' as discussed earlier. It is more likely the child will reduce or stop crying when there is nobody to witness it—no audience, no performance.

## Shopping (outing)

As we discussed earlier, when taking your child to the store, explain how you expect them to act while they are in the store with you. They are to walk next to you—no running away—while holding your hand or onto the wagon, or another object, if your hand is not available while walking in the parking lot. There should be no yelling/crying in the store; If you don't want to or plan on purchasing anything for your child, let them know in advance. If they are old enough, you can have them repeat the "rules" so they can have ownership. If they ask for an object while shopping, you can answer that with a question as discussed above: "Did we discuss that before we came into the store?" You can bring a toy or some snack for your child to focus on while the shopping is being done to avoid potential tantrums. If you have the time, let your child be a part of the experience: ask them to find the yellow package of bread, count four apples, find the bag that has the letter A, if they can read, find which aisle has the bread, etc. You can praise them along the way by saying, "I really like the way you're walking in the store next to me," "You're such a big helper!" Typically, the experience of going shopping is not that fun for children; do your best to make it quick.

## Sleeping in your bed

As a child, I remember the security I felt laying or sleeping between my parents during a thunderstorm—I never felt safer! When the child is sick or scared, many parents let their child sleep with them as well, which may inadvertently lead to an unwanted pattern. It is a personal choice but if it becomes excessive, it's harder to break the pattern. Continue your bedtime routine as always. When your child goes to bed after a book or whatever the routine is, it is possible they will ask for another book to delay the inevitable event of you giving them a kiss goodnight and leaving them. It is important to stick to the routine of saying goodnight and leaving the room; it is equally important **not** to return if your child tries to negotiate with you to come back. If your child comes to your bed in the middle of the night, do not say anything, just bring them back each time. It is important not to use any words as it provides reinforcement in the process.

## Social stories

Social stories explain certain social situations that your child may have difficulty facing. You can research a given topic online to find the following social stories or videos: fire drills, first /last day of school, how to share, adjust to eating lunch at school, speaking to others, feeling sad, feeling frustrated, social stories about being first, winning, losing, sharing, etc. If your child has apprehension about a possible social situation, such as a fire drill at school or the first day of school, you can look up the story online and print it out for your child. Read social stories to your child often to prepare them for the upcoming event. This can prepare them and anticipate actions to take when the moment arrives.

## Stages of Play:

0–3 months: Unoccupied Play
When a baby is making movements with their arms, legs, hands, and feet, they are learning about and discovering how their body moves and how they can control it.

0–2 years: Solitary Play
When a child plays alone and is not interested in playing with others quite yet.

2 years: Spectator/Onlooker Behavior
When a child watches and observes other children playing but will not play with them.

2+ years: Parallel Play
When a child plays alongside or near others but does not play with them directly.

3–4 years: Associate Play

When a child starts to interact with others during play, although there is not much cooperation required. For example, kids playing at the beach but doing different things.

## Stations

Children may need assistance in facilitating appropriate play at times. When you say to your child; "go play" they should have a few different, pre-planned activities to turn to called; stations. You should supervise your children as you create ample opportunity for them to explore appropriate developmental experiences that will foster their development. Set up a few different "stations" within their environment to explore a variety of opportunities. Examples may include: having a simple Artistic play, which may include: crayons, paper, glue sticks, gems, and stickers, or whatever you wish to add. An Abstract table can include: wooden square blocks, interlocking blocks, magnetic blocks, etc; to foster imaginary play. Pretend play can include: a kitchen area, tool set, dress up, or any functional life skills activities. An Academic table can include: manipulatives for math, such as unifix cubes, puzzles, matching games, and nesting objects. A Sensory table (for those who do not put objects in their mouth) and can be closely guarded, can include: play dough, kinetic sand, bean or rice bin with hidden treasures inside them, dried pasta, water play, etc. Use your imagination to switch up the stations as the children get older and their developmental stages change.

## Stuffing food

Stuffing food is dangerous and can lead to choking. If your child stuffs their mouth, you can limit the amount they take or limit what is offered. Always give them the opportunity to independently comply, but if necessary, a further step needs to be taken. For example, cut up the child's sandwich and tell them to take one piece at a time. If you do not want to cut the sandwich, then ask them to take one bite at a time. Instruct them that before taking another bite or piece, the first bite needs to be chewed and swallowed. First chew your food, then swallow it; after that, you can have another bite, until the sandwich or meal is complete. The alternative would be to let them see you cut up their food so they don't think they're missing out on any and keep the cut up food in front of you. Portion off the food to their plate, preferably one piece at a time, knowing they will stuff that in their mouth and continue the pattern of chewing and swallowing before obtaining more until the meal is complete. Gradually introduce more on the plate and monitor the action of your child, and either add more or take away depending on the level of progression made with slowing down the eating routine.

## Talking back

When asking your child to do something; do not accept any talking back; it may be effective to repeat the request again. Instead of yelling to your child about disrespect, simply repeat the request and you may add "what?" before you get the desired response. This may be beneficial if you ask your child to respond to your request. Let's give an example. If you ask your child to clean up their toys and they say, "No, I don't want to clean up!" repeat the request calmly. If they still choose not to clean up, ask them again. When your child says, "No," you can respond by asking, "What?" This pattern may continue until your child recognizes the original request. Just keep asking your child "what?" when they verbally challenge your request. This should make them confused, throwing them off their denial, which may result in them reconsidering their response—trickery!

## Tantrums

As stated earlier, behavior is a form of communication. It's also a part of children's development. That being said, tantrums are difficult to avoid at times. If you know your child is going to want to eat cookies throughout the day, put the cookies out of reach. Sometimes, out of sight is out of mind. You can redirect them by pulling out a favorite toy or give them something they can have instead (like fruit). This may result in the child dropping to the floor and crying, which is their way of saying they don't want the fruit. As long as your child is safe, it's best to implement the planned ignoring strategy as we discussed earlier, narrate what you're doing aloud, or simply walk away. If there is no audience, there is usually no performance. It's important not to talk to your child while they are in the middle of the tantrum, as this may result in them getting louder and prolonging the tantrum and may interfere with self-soothing and coping skills. It is equally important not to give them the object that started the tantrum in the first place (the cookie). This creates boundaries that are necessary for discipline, as well as being consistent when telling them "no."

## Teachable moments

Teachable moments happen naturally—it's the perfect opportunity when you can capitalize on a functional, ordinarily occurring situation and it's relevant in the moment. For example, when you're at a special event like a petting zoo, it's appropriate to discuss animals and their sounds/environment. When you're in a public place, stress the importance of holding hands in the parking lot (it's dangerous if they run), and staying next to you while in the store (it can be unsafe to be around strangers), etc. When you're playing with your child with blocks, which may happen to have letters on them, it's not a teachable moment to drill them about labeling the letters, unless they initiate it. Instead focus on the joy of building and having fun. It may get boring for your child if you're constantly trying to "teach" your child while you engage with them. Focus more on laughing with your child instead of being their instructor. You can play games with your child if you'd like to teach them while engaging; for learning colors and shapes: say; "let's look around the room/park/dinner table to see if we can find colors and shapes." As they get older you can adapt to looking for items that start with the letter "B" and so on.

## Terminology

It is important to use correct terminology while talking with your child. Use simple, novel words like: "wait," "stop," "no," "go play," "Mommy's on the phone right now, you need to wait," and other directed actions or words that children need to hear in order to respect the environment they're in. Sometimes children need to be self-sufficient—playing solo while waiting for attention. If your child chooses not to comply with a specific request, they may need some assistance. For example, one line I like to use is, "I heard Mommy ask you to clean up. If I heard her, I'm sure you did, too!" Always give your child the opportunity to comply on their own, but if they need assistance in executing the original request, you can use hand over hand. "I heard Daddy ask you to wash your hands for dinner. If I heard him, I'm sure you did, too." If they do not comply, assist in the action by accompanying them to the bathroom, reminding them to remember to be a good listener as you assist in washing their hands. This ties in to boundaries—children do not control the environment they are in, the parent does. I will reiterate that consistency and being on the same team, as parents, cannot be compromised—Mom and Dad need to be on the same page today and in the future.

## Throwing

Throwing objects across the room may be a common action among children who are angry or impulsive. It can also be just active play. It goes back to a previous statement in this book about choosing your battles: was it intentional or was it unintended? If it was intentional, ask your child to "go pick it up" immediately. As discussed previously, give your child an opportunity to comply with your request before you use a physical prompt (walking them over to the area and using hand over hand to pick up the object). You can count to three to give your child an additional opportunity to comply with your request if they choose not to. Say, "I'll count to three. Hopefully, you'll make the right choice to pick it up. If not, I'll "help" you."

Start counting aloud to three and if your child is not making an attempt to retrieve the thrown object, by the time you get to three, you should be on your feet. Without using any words, take your child to the thrown object—walk them over to it either by holding their hand or if they keep dropping to the floor, put your hands under their armpits from behind them to assist them in walking. The last resort would be to carry them until they get to the destination of the thrown object. Once the thrown object is picked up; by either the child willingly or by you providing hand over hand support, bring it back to its original destination. If your child is protesting, use no words with the exception of singing the clean-up song. Place no focus on the child's behavior at this time, just the task at hand.

# Time-out

The general rule for time-out durations is to match the child's age in minutes. There is no specific destination for a time-out—it could be on the steps, chair, couch, floor, etc. The important thing to remember is to give a warning before the child is to be put in time-out—it gives them the chance to redirect their own behavior. However, if your child is physically inappropriate towards any individual or animal, then time-out needs to be immediate. There should be NO talking to your child while the child is in time-out. If they run out of the designated spot, say nothing, just direct them back and start the time from the beginning. It would be helpful to use a visual–an hourglass or an auditory timer so the child can monitor how long before their time-out is over. It is voluntary, but it may have the child obtain ownership if you ask them why they went into time-out if they are able to communicate. Prompt them if necessary and if they are developmentally able, ask how they could have handled the situation differently. Some parents want an apology but the only drawback to that is that you can't control whether your child talks. If they refuse to say, "sorry," then what? It's a good idea to avoid it if you don't think your child will comply with the verbal "sorry" request. Remember, after time-out is completed, there should be no grudges. Use a simple gesture like a hug to let them know that there are no repercussions after the time-out. It is important to consider that if a child's behavior does not begin to decrease with the time-out practice, you may have to consider a different consequence.

## Transitioning

Transitions can be difficult for toddlers because it means switching from one activity to another (often sooner than they want it to be.) Transitions are important in order to move on to other things throughout the day. It should be a smooth, unrushed, and well-organized transition so that moving to the next step gradually avoids stressful situations. For example, "In five minutes, we need to get dressed for dance," "In two minutes, it's time to hit pause on the iPad to eat lunch," "After the show is over, it's time for bed." Remember to be consistent in your approach, otherwise it sends mixed messages to your child.

## Turn off button

Children engaged in a fun activity or frolic play typically don't want it to end. They don't have a "turn off button" and need ample reminders that playtime is limited and will end soon. There are a few different ways to prepare them for the completion of the activity, such as by saying, "two more minutes," "one more time," "when the song is over," "when the timer stops, we will be done with (the activity)." Then end the activity when the time is up. Stick to your original cutoff time. You can always resume at a different time just not in that moment; this is an example of setting boundaries.

## TV

In my experience, I have had parents who don't let their children watch TV at all and I've had parents tell me that they can sit their child in front of the TV on a Sunday and watch *Toy Story*, all four shows, in one afternoon, which adds up to approximately eight hours. Television should not be a "babysitter" and it certainly should not be controlled by a toddler, meaning the toddler does not decide at all times what channel to put watch. If other family members want to watch something other than what the child wants to watch, then it's up to the parents to redirect the child by having a play bin filled with toys for the child to play with instead of watching TV.

# u

## Unconditional love

There are times when parents say, "They don't listen to me like they listen to you!" Or "As soon as I bring him/her home, they act out," or "He/she is well-behaved at school and then he/she comes home and it's like they're a different child." There is no definitive answer. My theory is that it is as simple as the unconditional love that parents have for their children. Home is the child's domain, where they feel most comfortable and can be themselves without worrying that they won't be accepted for who they are. I like to tell parents to take it as a compliment that the child feels they can be themselves without judgment!

## Using words for your children; if they can't or won't

I often hear parent's utter: "Say you're sorry!" If there's one thing you cannot control it is whether your child will speak when asked. I advise parents to "use words for them" (their children) in certain situations. If your child grabs another child—whether it is hitting or biting—and upon your request, won't say "sorry," it may be effective to practice the planned ignoring strategy coupled with saying sorry FOR them. "I'm sorry (name) (fill in the action) you; that was not acceptable/nice/kind (whatever word you choose)" while you turn your back to the aggressor and address the victim. This is what it looks like: Say, "I'm sorry, Johnny hit you, that's not kind" while you put your attention on the person that was targeted. This can be done in pet scenarios: "I'm sorry (pet; child's name) pulled your tail, that's not acceptable." Another example: "I'm sorry, Johnny took that toy away from you," as you have Johnny hand it back (hand over hand) if necessary. Children model behavior; if this is what they see, the goal is for them to act that way in the future. Set appropriate examples.

## Utensils

Children love their "finger foods" and are encouraged to use their fingers when they are younger to grasp snacks such as cereal, snacks, cut up food, and fruit. As they develop, they are expected to advance to using appropriate utensils to replace their fingers. Encourage children to use forks and spoons as they develop an interest in advanced foods that require such utensils. Use hand over hand and assist in stabbing with a fork if necessary, as well as bringing food and liquid to your child's mouth with a spoon. Continue to place utensils in your child's hand to discourage using fingers instead of a more advanced form of eating with a fork or a spoon.

# V

## Validating feelings

It is impossible to know what another person is feeling. However, it IS possible to validate their feelings instead of dismissing them. It's how individuals act out their feelings that may require some redirection at times. Some simple examples of feeling and reactions include feeling scared of a spider and running away screaming, feeling happy to see someone and hugging them, feeling sad and crying, feeling angry and shouting. Those are pretty straightforward and the actions accompanying them may apply to examples stated above. There are some examples of feelings that are much harder to detect—a child with feeling frustrated that they are unable to get their point across; possibly a language delay, feeling that they don't want to share their toys with their bothersome younger sibling, feeling that they are scared to be in an unfamiliar environment. These examples are harder to detect, and the behaviors associated with them may differ from typical behaviors, which vary from child to child. As we discussed earlier, behavior is a form of communication. If a child acts his feelings out in an inappropriate manner, it is important to identify the feeling first, then address the unwanted behavior. For example, "I see that you're angry that your sister broke your car but you are not allowed to push her," "I can see that you're frustrated (at getting his/her language out to communicate their needs). Can you show me what you want?" Or "I understand that you are scared and I see all your friends here (daycare) remember, mommy always comes back to pick you up." Let your child know that you are able to validate their feelings and they may be more willing to discuss them going forward, if they are able. They need to know and understand that you are in their corner and perhaps there may be an unspoken language you can read when the time is right and an intervention is needed.

## Visual prompts

We've discussed prompting earlier to assist with transitions and routines. Visual prompting is taking it a step further to help ensure that your child understands patterns and to familiarize transitions in an appropriate way, by way of pictures and sometimes the actual objects. Whether it is offering a choice between an array of two items from the refrigerator or the snack cabinet, toy preference or TV/movie, present two choices for what they can have and simply ask, "Which one?" Depending on your child's cognitive/language ability, they can either: look at an item, point to the desired object, or label the desired food item. Visual prompting consists of having the child either point at or request verbally for the pictures previously taken and printed of objects to assist in transitioning or to obtain what the child desires. For example, take pictures of all the items in the refrigerator that the child eats. Have a display of those items on a poster board or folder, attached with velcro to the folder, and attach it to the designated area—to the refrigerator. The child then can either point to the desired food that they would like to eat; (pictures should be within the vicinity of their interest) pictures of objects that are in the refrigerator should be posted on the refrigerator, pictures of ice cream, ice pops should be on the freezer. Or if it has velcro attached, they can take it off the board and hand it to you—and there is your communication instead of anticipating their needs. This can be done with the child's recreation area. Label each toy bin with pictures that are in that bin. For daily schedules, take pictures of each task or event that will occur that day. For example: Night-time routine picture boards may look like pictures (previously taken) of your child eating dinner, a picture of your TV, a picture of their toys for play, a picture of the bathtub, a picture of the child's toothbrush, a picture of books, and a picture of their bed. However you choose to arrange the pictures, it's a visual reminder for the child that a routine is followed, which will assist in their participation and help them deal with difficulties in following their morning, daily, or night-time routines.

## Walking feet

Part of a child's tantrum may include dropping to the floor. If you are in the middle of a transition at the time and they drop to the floor in protest, pick the child up off the floor and plant his/her feet on the ground and tell them, "Walking feet." Do not carry your child to the targeted destination. Place your hands under their armpits for assistance to hoist them up and use your feet, placed directly behind theirs, to move their feet forward. Continue to use the phrase, "Walking feet," as you move across the floor until the child is walking independently.. Praise them by saying, "Nice job walking to the (destination) all by yourself."

## Warnings

I've walked into houses to treat a student and have witnessed caregivers yank away an iPad or toy or turn off the TV as soon as I walk in the door and then they tell the child that it's "learning time." Naturally this leads to the child being upset and crying—as it would upset you too! There are many times when I give the child back the iPad/toy or turn the TV back on and give the child a calm end of activity warning: "One more song," "two more minutes," "when the hourglass runs out of sand," etc. It gives the child an indication that the end is near for their particular use of entertainment. Then I either ask the child to turn off the TV themselves or to voluntarily hand over the iPad when the allotted time is up. If they do not voluntarily give up the toy or turn off the TV, hand over hand may be applied. When you take your child to an outing, give them a warning before you leave and stick to your original plan, don't let your child talk you into additional turns or more time. That's all part of being consistent and following through.

What could your child have done differently?

For those children who are more aware of how their behavior may affect others, a good way to foster empathy is to ask: what could you have done differently (in the way they handled a situation)? It gets the child thinking about how to best handle the way they react to adverse or even positive situations in a more responsible way. For example, a child is playing with her dolls and her younger sibling comes along and takes one of the dolls. The reaction of the child is to push her sibling and grab the doll back and yell, "Mine!" This causes the sibling to cry and makes the child feel bad. When reflecting with your child about their behavior, it's ok to help with suggestions for how they could have handled the situation differently. Together you can come up with different scenarios and how to best react going forward.

Which one?

There is a stage of children's lives where they want to be independent and control areas of their life but are not fully capable of doing so. It becomes too overwhelming to make a choice when there is an abundance of options. If you want your child to be able to make their own choices, give them a choice of two things, and ask, "Which one?" This will foster their independence without the chaos of too many objects to choose from.

To the children that are language-delayed and cannot communicate their needs, you can present them with the same strategy. Display two choices, and ask, "Which one?" For example, at breakfast time, show them the box of frozen waffles and a box of cereal, then ask the question and have them point to the desired object. You can then say, "Nice choice picking the waffles for breakfast." It's important to label the objects for the children, so that they understand that words have meaning. This can be done with: toys, books, TV choices, snacks, and anything functional during daily activities.

"Why?"

Some children will repeatedly ask "why?" Don't get in the habit of repeating your answer over and over again. After you have answered the question once, you ask them "why?" when they ask the same question. You can remind them that you have already answered the question and give them a chance to recall the answer. For example, "Why can't I have candy?" The original answer was "You can have candy after lunch." Ask your child, "Why can't you have candy?" They should be able to answer the question; if not, remind them with clues by asking, "When can you have candy?" This strategy should stop the general inquiry throughout the day.

# Working from home

Since the pandemic, there are parents that are working from home and are not able to give direct care to their children, even though an alternative adult is available to care for the child. I've witnessed parents going into an office and expecting their children to understand that they are working and are not to be disturbed. Children don't understand that at all; what they know is that Mommy or Daddy are home and behind closed doors, and they want to be in their vicinity. They don't comprehend that they just can't barge in at their leisure to spend time with them. One way that may stop an unexpected barge-in is to put a green piece of paper, on the outside of the door, when it's ok for the door to be open and putting a red piece of paper, on the door, for when the door cannot be opened. You can switch up the visual aid to a green traffic light and a red traffic light, a green sign that says "go" and a red "stop" sign, whatever works for your child! Practice the action of opening the door on green and stopping at the door on red until your child understands the meanings; then you will be able to implement the new strategy.

# Winding down

It makes sense to have calming activities within the hour so the child is in a relaxed state before getting ready to go down for a nap or when it's almost bedtime or mealtime. There are many activities that promote this state—soft music, reading books, soothing bath, watching TV, doing puzzles. Some parents like to drive their children until they fall asleep and then transfer them into their beds, rocking in a rocking chair. Whatever is calming to your child, it's best to introduce that activity before you want them to be able to settle down for a meal or a nap.

## Working hard

If you got a paycheck at the end of the week for doing nothing, why would you want to work? If a child got whatever they wanted without having to earn it, why would they work hard to earn anything? If you anticipate a child's needs and they don't have to ask for food/drink, they won't use their words. Children need to earn rewards, use their words to get their needs met, if they are able, and that's how we obtain desired objects, confidence, and self-esteem!

## X marks the spot

There are homes that I go into that have scribbled crayon on the walls, stickers on the windows, marker drawings on the doors, etc. Have your child clean up the walls, windows, and doors. Even if they don't get it all, it makes them take ownership for the inappropriate markings. Use hand over hand if necessary and tell them that they need to use those materials on paper or something else besides the walls, windows, or any other parts of the house. If your child purposely spills water or throws food on the floor, have them clean it up or pick it up. It's probably much more fun for a child to watch their caregiver clean up after them than to have to do it themselves. Be consistent with having them take accountability for their actions and it should lessen the behavior.

## Yelling

The more you yell, the more the likelihood that you will be tuned out. It also sends the message that you are not in control of your own actions as a parent/caregiver, which escalates anxiety and behavior. I've witnessed parents that yell and it is not effective if it's done all the time. Speaking firmly if your child is being non-compliant can be a different alternative. If you whisper at times, maybe you'll trick your child into tuning in to more of what you have to say.

## You're doing the best that you can

You may not be doing everything right, but nobody does it like you! You have the best interests of your child in mind and that's what counts. Keep a positive attitude and keep putting one foot in front of the other!

## Zany

Be silly, be animated, dance, laugh, and sing. The more outlandish the message, the better it is received by children.

## Zero tolerance

Please do not allow your children to harm your pets, ignore you, or be aggressive to anyone in your household. If your child pesters or hurts your pet and gets hurt in the process, it's not the animal's fault; it's your child's fault. If you allow your child to ignore you as a toddler, it will give them control over you. If you don't give a consequence for aggression, it may escalate. Do not walk on eggshells around your child; be calm, be firm, and give immediate consequences for undesired behaviors and model appropriate behaviors.

There are very specific guidelines to follow when deciding to start a behavior plan with your child/children. It's very hard to change a behavior that has been well-established but the sooner the better; the window of opportunity starts to close the longer one waits. Typically speaking, however long the behavior is displayed, is how long it takes to alter. My experience differs from that, however. Once demands are placed on a child that has already been displaying inappropriate conduct, they will get very angry about you suddenly trying to change that behavior and they will INCREASE the intensity of their inappropriate behavior, in hopes that you will back off and let them continue as things were; nobody likes change! This is a critical part in the process; stay consistent, follow through, and the behaviors—if it's not a neurological condition—should decrease. The one time you're tired or not in the mood to deal with undesired actions and give in, is the time it will start all over again as your child will have learned that you will give in if they're persistent. That sends mixed messages to your child; therefore it's unfair to them. Once you make the commitment to start, follow through; you may see changes quite quickly.

Now you have some basic knowledge on how to implement strategies to combat undesired behaviors, in order to have a household full of laughter, love, and (of course) discipline! I used to say about my own children, "I may not do everything right but nobody does it like me." You're your child's biggest fan, even though sometimes you don't want to cheer for them at their worst; consider it a compliment that they feel like they can be themselves with the knowledge that they're loved unconditionally!

If you are consistent in your approach, then baby steps will eventually lead to running a marathon!!

The very best to you always!

For: questions, clarification, or comments please email me @ lionheartedcoaching@gmail.com

To make an appointment to assist in implementing effective coaching strategies; please visit my website @ lionheartedcoaching.org